CW00338974

WHITE EAGLE'S
LITTLE BOOK
OF ANGELS

WHITE EAGLE'S

Little Book of Angels

WHITE EAGLE PUBLISHING TRUST

NEW LANDS · LISS · HAMPSHIRE · ENGLAND

www.whiteaglepublishing.org

First published 2010

British Library Cataloguing in Publication Data
A catalogue entry for this book is available from the
British Library
ISBN 978-0-85487-208-4

© *Copyright, The White Eagle Publishing Trust, 2010*
Illustrations © Margaret Bentley, 2010

Set in Ehrhardt at the Publisher and
Printed by National Press, Amman, Jordan

CONTENTS

*T*HE ANGELS *work ceaselessly to uplift humanity. There can be no separation between angels and human beings; they work together side by side. This universal brotherhood, this brotherhood with the angels, is continually being welded and strengthened. May we be simple and pure in heart, and so receptive to the Messengers, the Angelic Ones. May the inflow of the spirit of love prepare the way.*

1

Working with Angels

FROM the great archangel at the head of each ray, down to the most insignificant nature spirit, the universe is seething with invisible life. Within such a cloud of unseen witnesses you live and have your being!

You hear of angels visiting the seers and prophets of old, but you do not always realize that angels are always working among the human family. At the present time the vibration of the angelic life forces is what humanity needs to restore correct balance. We should seek the inspiration of the angels of light and ask that they work with us; the individual can do so much to help the angelic ones in their work of raising the vibrations of earth.

When a human being sits devotedly in meditation and contemplation and opens his or her heart to the inflow of divine Love, that being will be so raised in consciousness as to behold the angels of God. The lowly soul will reach that state of ecstasy and glory in which he or she will be in company with angels. Here is the true spiritual gift. Here is the true goal, my friends, and it is far more than the development of any sixth sense or psychic power.

You know how, through the expansion of your consciousness, you have gained help. You may do much more than this; you may fight within yourself to retain supremacy over the animal instincts and the darkness and depression of the earth life. You may carry with you an optimism about life.... More than this, you may carry a positive knowledge—positive thought and positive action—as you journey through life, and thus train your spiritual hearing to catch the words of power and truth broadcast from the heights.

You will get there: you will get to the joy and the happiness of that glorious realization of the beauty of the natural world. You will discover, beyond all the conflict and darkness of earth, a wise purpose working through the chaos and taking you into a world of brotherhood and peace. Be ready for a golden world and a golden age. Keep this ideal before you and it will help you.

The Angels, the Messengers of God, are waiting to guide you toward the temple of wisdom and instruction, and if you go with them you will absorb all this wisdom.

To be of service, you must visualize those forces and identify yourself with this vast company of shining spirits. You must feel that you are part of this company, you must visualize the angels. Look up, look up!

You are ringed about with angelic brethren. Put your hand into the hand of the angel by your side.

If you raise your consciousness above the fears and turmoil of the earth, it is like ascending from a fog into a layer of peace and beauty. It is like quitting a wilderness grown barren and ugly and stunted, and following a path into a garden fragrant with flowers and the song of birds and running water—beautified by sunlight and by the colour of flowers and trees.

You become attuned to the creative spheres as you begin to become aware of what is taking place inside you, as you live with your eyes open. You see always beauty and never destruction; you begin to see with the eyes of your spirit the beauty in nature and within all the elements. And as you perhaps start to follow your soul's urge towards some creative art, angels from those creative spheres are drawn to you; they watch your work and inspire and guide you.

The angels, the messengers of God, are waiting to guide you toward the temple of wisdom and instruction, and if you go with them you will absorb all this wisdom into your higher mind. In time it will percolate through into your everyday, ordinary mind. But you will have to train yourself. If you take one or two falls, and feel disappointed, never mind. The first step is to listen to the little voice within. Through this you will develop such a pure 'sounding board' within that you will hear the angels sing....

THE PROCESS

Manifest the higher life in your own being. Look up to the Light and pray to become greater channels for the Light. It does no good to dwell on darkness. Be still. Unless there is stillness within, the angels cannot work for you. If you become the prey of violent emotions or desires, the finer angelic vibrations fail to be transmitted. Be therefore still if you would seek the angels.

Every day, before you start your daily work, practise this—even if only for five minutes. Send your thoughts to those in spirit, both human and angelic, who watch and help you. Let this spiritual life become alive for you, so that it is always with you. May every day of life find you opening the windows, not only of your home but of your soul, to let the sunlight flood you. When you 'open' in this way, you will grow in wellbeing, in the power to love, in kindliness to life. As the power grows more potent, so you will become more assured as to this invisible force, its reality and effect.

AFFIRMATIONS FOR WORKING WITH ANGELS

I open my heart and my soul to the angels.

*I am in the light, and am
filled with the light.*

*The angels work with me to bring
light to the world.*

*T*HE *guardian angel is there to inspire, guide and help us on our path through life. We retain freewill, but can become attuned to the angelic influences that lead towards the Light. A personal, close relationship of guidance can be achieved through regular contact with our own angel.*

2

The Guardian Angel

DO NOT forget that you have a guardian angel ready at your prayer to draw close and to help you in your task of serving humankind. There is with every human soul, always, the teacher, the guide; always, the guardian angel. And so there is such a thing as spiritual guidance, not only through the innermost being, and not only through the inner light, but by guardian angels in the beyond. Many are responding unconsciously to such guidance. The time will come when you will one and all respond to the influence of your guardian angel.

Every one of you here has your own guide and angel helpers, and the person in the street, whether he accepts it or not, whether she will or not, still has his or her guardian angel. The lowest of us has yet a pure guardian angel watching, who sees—beneath the squalor of body and even soul, and maybe ever so faintly—the spirit, the little glimmer of light. This angel is ever trying to fan that flame, and to give encouragement and help to the flickering light.

At the time of a person's birth, and even before the actual birth, the guardian angel is at work. The moment that the soul takes the decision to reincarnate, it comes under the care of the guardian angel. That guardian angel remains with the soul during the whole of its life, and when the soul passes onward, the guardian angel receives the soul in the spirit world.

The guardian angel works under the direction of the Lords of Karma, because the soul in its charge has come back in order to pay its karmic debts and thereby to clear certain lessons. By contrast, the guardian angel is not of the human kingdom. It is concerned with the karma of the soul in its charge, and helps to bring about certain conditions in the soul's life. The guardian angel is impersonal in this respect; it supervises the learning of certain lessons, and it watches over birth, marriage, death, for it is above all concerned with these big karmic events.

The guardian angel is there to inspire, guide and help but never to force the soul. No guide, whether human or angelic, may do this. The soul, having freewill, may decide its own course within limits, and the human being's gift of freewill is always respected. The soul must choose, but at the same time it may feel the helpful influence of the guardian angel. Many, many times the guardian angel draws close to the soul entrusted to its care, but when that soul is so concerned with the world and with itself, it cannot receive the guidance.

You see the value of the development of the quiet mind, the steady soul? You must be aware of spirit life. You must learn to become receptive to the guardian angel, receptive to spiritual thought, spiritual ideas. Ask for guidance, particularly when you fall to sleep at night, and be on the alert for impressions in the early morning. Answers will be dropped into your minds. You will be amazed at the true guidance and help forthcoming.

Never forget: you do not walk alone, for your guardian angel is helping you in every endeavour. Whenever you are ready to know more, you will certainly learn more. Be of good courage, and never forget your guardian angel. Do not be afraid, whatever your challenge. Nothing can hurt you if you resign yourself to the love of God. May you be attuned to the heavenly sounds: sensitive to the presence of the guardian angels, the unseen messengers from the realms of light and love. Some day you will see your angel revealed, wondrous and beautiful: the one who has been standing beside you with outspread wings, helping in your evolution.

When you fall asleep, let your mind be calm and still. Think of the hush over the earth. All nature sleeps. Put yourself into rhythm with nature. In like manner all nature awaits the coming, the baptism of the sun. Then will you be released harmoniously, and your guardian angel at your side will take your hand and lead you forth to one of the many temples that exist on the etheric plane. And there you will receive instruction, and your soul will be impressed so vividly that some of the experiences will remain in your waking moments.

THE PROCESS

In order to calm the mind when you are ready for sleep, take a few deeper breaths. As you breathe in, imagine that you are filling your body with the essence of the angel of peace. As you breathe out, feel yourself surrendering into softness, comfort, warmth and belonging, just as your body relaxes into the cocoon of your bed. Feel the skin on your face loosen, and have the sensation that your eyes are softening and spreading out, allowing the inner gaze to become unfocused. Imagine you are letting your mind drift, so that when thoughts and feelings arise, they simply pass by or through without attention. Allow yourself to feel detached from life, yet completely safe in God's embrace. Just at that moment when your consciousness is released, you can become aware of the strong, still presence of your guardian angel ready to take you home.

*I am open and ready to receive
guidance from my angel.*

*Angelic influences flow through me
and bring me close to God.*

*My angel is always by my side
and is ready to guide me.*

*A*BOVE and around us all are the radiant beings of the higher worlds. The angels of healing and harmony gather round. Those who are
troubled shall find peace, and those who are sick
shall be healed; those in the darkness shall see light.

3

Healing Angels

THINK of angels in your healing work, because only the angels have the inner knowledge which the human mind needs but is unable to grasp and use. The angels of healing work under the Christ Ray: they work under the Master Jesus, and are full of compassion, tenderness and love. They bring to humanity, when it needs it, the healing substances, which may also be described as fine threads of light. They are very radiant. Some are clothed in one particular colour, others in many colours. Sometimes the group will come purely on one colour ray, and sometimes the group will be in pure white.

It is not possible to describe the harmony

and the perfume which these angels bring. On earth at present, little is known about these angels of healing, but as the age advances many more people will not only feel the presence of angelic beings, they will know how to call upon them and they will see them. By prayer and pure thought, angels are drawn to your aid. By simplicity of spirit and purity of body and soul in those who participate, the angels can work more powerfully.

Picture a great ray of light coming down, full of angel forms. There is a ray of gold, a ray of rose, a ray of soft amethyst, and a ray of pure yellow. Visualize in each ray countless forms with the semblance of a human face.... We speak of the ministering angels who work purely with these cosmic rays of life. Picture then the other angel beings who stand around the patient, pouring forth love and perfume and enfolding him or her in music. Angels, in forms both human and heavenly, work together to pour forth the power of healing.

You will see the most delicate colours of the rainbow moving, vibrating, in beautifully soft, billow-like clouds, and see beings standing with folded wings all around the place in which you do your healing work.

You should try to be very still and silent. Aspire to a silence not only of the physical body, but a mental, emotional and spiritual silence. Be still in mind and body, and surrender absolutely to this spiritual healing power. Then will come great beings who are the angels of healing. They are still, and are directing rays of light which go forth from their heads, from their aura. They are not disturbed by any world problem. They know one truth, that all is working together for good, and they come to help humanity realize this one grand truth: *all is working together for good.*

When the body is healed, when the angels help to purify and perfect the physical body, they do more than this. They create. They weave into the subtler vehicles, and into the actual physical form, forces and light and spiritual power. Not only do these forces assist the healing of the patient in this life, but they are destined slowly but surely to create and make ready the human form for the next race. Behind any individual ministration by the healing angels, there is always the grand plan of building for the future of life. So while the angels work always for this object, you, in simplicity and humility, also work for the future. By opening the channel and building up the necessary vibrations of thought, you are greatly assisting not only the individual, but the whole evolution of humanity.

ATTUNING TO THE ANGELS OF HEALING

You are surrounded by the angels. You may not be able to see them, but you may be able to feel them. They are with you, in the quiet of your own innermost being.

Do a simple ritual. Try to be very still and silent, espouse a silence not only of the physical body, but a mental, emotional and spiritual silence too. Be still in mind and body, and surrender absolutely to this spiritual healing power. Then, by the simple ritual you have performed, you draw to yourself the angels of healing.

These angel beings draw very close to you. You help to build the bridge across which the angels come.

Never forget the angels by your side. Hold the hand of love and true humility in your work. 'Lord: of myself I can do nothing. It is your life force which is in me. It is your life force that guides my brain. It is your life force that gives me strength to work manually, mentally, spiritually.'

We see the great canopy of white wings. They are alive, and are not made of plaster: they are living wings, pulsating with light all over this shrine, this temple in the spirit world.* We are right up in the mountain tops and the air we breathe is pure and fresh. As we enter the portals of the temple, angels stand one on either side like two pillars. As we pass them we are offered the cup of pure water, the grail cup.

Sip! Sip the water of life, the healing water, and enter this holy place. We are in a golden world, and we see all round in a circle angel forms with wings of light. We see beautiful faces, all so perfectly peaceful and joyous. You can feel the joy, you can feel the peace, you feel your troubles and your heaviness all falling away.

*In the London White Eagle Lodge, where we believe this teaching was given, there is a plaster model of the outspread wings of an eagle.

We look about us, and that dome of wings is supported by tall pillars of light, and each pillar is a great healing angel. We feel this power, this healing, this beautiful blessing.

If you are true to God and yourself, you are taking part in a true ceremony, a true service of healing.

HEALING AFFIRMATIONS WITH THE ANGELS

The angels of healing draw close and pour their light through me.

I am attuned to the radiant power of the healing angels.

God's healing light flows through me and into me.

A VAST sphere of life interpenetrates this earth life, guiding and working and helping onward the great plan of spiritual evolution. Not only is this unseen life working through the physical manifestations of earth, but it is also linked to other planets. There are angelic and planetary beings working with one object, which is to project, through their will, rays of light to penetrate the minds of all humanity.

4

Planetary Angels

WE WANT you to understand the importance of the planetary influences, of the communion which links all earth's humanity to the angels. You do not live and work alone: you are part of the elements, part of heaven itself. You and all people are upheld by the projection of these rays of light, of love and power, which are being continually sent to you. When a soul can contact and receive these rays, it will gain assistance from angel beings.

We have on occasions described to you some of the ceremonies of the past, when the ancient brethren paced their vast temple or lodge, which lay under open sky, lit by myriad stars. Light from other planets, both seen and unseen, fell gently upon their vast gathering. All present understood that they were gathered to worship under the direction of the angels of the light, and when the first streaks of dawn became visible, a great hush fell upon the assembly, a great stillness. When the first rays of the sun appeared and day was born, these peoples turned to the light—worshipping, praising, thanking the Great White Spirit for the coming of the new day.

The ancient people understood that in these ceremonies they were touching the very heart of life and the secret of power. They knew at that moment that they were not only receiving into their being the radiation of the sun, but that they were being strengthened and purified. They breathed in the Light, which was an actual life force: a purifier, perfector and glorifier of human life. This knowledge of the power and life emanating from the great Light was handed down through the ages.

Those who have studied the ancient science of astrology know by their studies that it is true. They know that planetary influences have an effect upon the individual and upon the world. This is only a part of the tremendous influence guiding and working through the affairs of the world, and the souls of men and women. We cannot find words to impress upon you the mighty spiritual forces which are playing upon humanity.

We would have you know that planetary angels, planetary messengers are watching. Surrounding you and circling you are the lesser angels and the great angels, and rays from the great planetary angels, the angels from the seven sacred planets. The messengers from the planets are drawn to humanity, bringing an ancient and eternal truth. When all humanity understands and lives this truth, you will be able to draw upon vast powers in the universe for good, for beauty, for perfection of life. You will begin to understand the invisible power behind life, the power which is at work.

Have no fear; all things are working together for good. Leave the great angels to know their work, for all will bring good.

CONTACTING THE PLANETARY ANGELS

We would like first to open your consciousness to the presence of the angel beings. We would concentrate or focus your thoughts upon the angels.

Try to forget that you are men and women. Try to realize that you are spirit, and in the presence of a large company of spirit beings: radiant beings of the earth stream of life, and shining angels. Whatever you think about, whatever you do in your daily lives, we beg you to concentrate upon love and harmony always. Love and work from your heart—not so much from the brain!

We want to ask you again to practise the

holy breathing—the slow, rhythmic, calm, relaxed breathing—and at the same time, forgetting the earth, to rise up, up, up in aspiration to the world above. Aspire to the world of spirit life, which is a world of Light, and a place where all souls live in the full consciousness of the true life. This is the God life, for there the people walk and talk with angels.

Remember there are angels in attendance all the time. Shining spirit forms are with you and, by the power which is created here, you are raised in consciousness. If you concentrate and give all your simple faith to the work, you can become *en rapport* with the angels on higher planes, and in other worlds and other planets.

THE PROCESS

We would open before you a vista of infinite joy, where the soul is completely free from contact with the earth....

Look up, my children, into the night sky and see the host of shining stars. Pause and wonder what these stars are. Think of yourself and your companions, brethren of the light, having the power, the freedom to move among the stars, from planet to planet. Think of shining, apparently winged beings, moving in the heavens into light and more light with greater freedom and greater comprehension of this universe and of universes beyond this small universe. There are planets of light and spiritual glory beyond your understanding, to which souls go. *Eye hath not seen, nor ear heard* the glory of the heavenly life, the God life to which all God's children are heirs.

Onward into the life more abundant and glorious than your little earth-mind can conceive! Seek first the kingdom of God and then all will be made clear to you.

AFFIRMATIONS WITH THE PLANETARY ANGELS

*I am open to the beauty and power
of the infinite universe.*

*The angels guide and direct the
avenues of my life.*

The power of the planets flows through me.

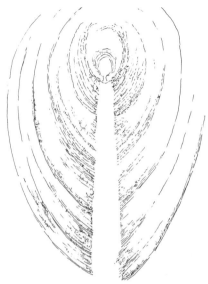

WHAT a glorious world! We see all around you the forms of angelic beings, waiting to serve, to fill your souls with love and peace.... Through aspiration and attunement you can be released and see, with the eye of truth and illumination, the interblending of all life. You will see the companies of angels, of nature spirits and of devas, and thus become yourself a recreated and regenerated being.

5

Angels of Earth

YOU MAY not have realized before what an important place the natural world holds in the grand scheme of life. There is no such thing in all creation as splendid isolation; no separation between any forms of life. All are blended in one harmonious whole. Those who are referred to as angelic hierarchies or devas are concerned with the evolution and the building of form in nature. The angelic ones are concerned with the building of vehicles or forms in every realm of life. The angelic realm is on earth. As the human realm stands in relation to the mineral, so stands the angelic in relation to the human realm.

Hidden in the rocks, the stones, the seas, the skies and all the nature kingdom lies the kingdom of the angels.

You are learning about the wondrous love of God and the organization or the plan of the masters. The great masters and their angelic servers, all of them, work in mind and heart and hand for the development of human life, its growth and the ultimate perfecting. When a seed is sown in mother earth it does not shoot up instantly. It has to mature, gradually unfold. It has to penetrate the darkness of the soil. It has to appear above the soil and then reach up to the sunlight. In due time, the glorious flower comes into bloom—to give so much pleasure. Later on, when the flower has finished, then there develops the fruit. Now this is such an excellent example of the way God, or spirit, works in human life, and of what you are learning as you gradually work through your karma and learn your lessons.

The ancients were taught how to work with the angels to control the elements. They learnt how to make contact mentally and spiritually with the forces of nature, and how to use them, and live and work in harmony with them. The brothers in those days were taught to breathe in consciously; to meditate on nature, on the beauty of the grass and the corn and the flowers and the trees and all the blessings of nature. They were taught how, in the act of breathing in the fresh air, they could also establish contact with the angels of light. Therefore these angelic or nature forces were able to direct rays of light, power, wisdom and love to the brothers; and through certain practices—notably in meditation and in their way of life—they were able to form very true and beautiful links with those natural forces, and even with the great devas themselves.

As you unfold spiritually, you will be able to see, just as the ancients did, the angels associated with the earth element. We want you all gradually to understand and learn the power of creative thought, God thought. We want you to understand and work in harmony with natural and spiritual laws, which govern all life. We want you to learn to thank God for every manifestation of these laws, even if to do so sometimes seems dark and difficult. Remember, without the rain you would have no harvest, and would wither and die. You have to learn to understand and accept the natural laws as the ancients did, to love and rejoice in the rain as well as the sunshine. This is a secret which is most important for humanity to learn.

CONTACTING THE ANGELS OF EARTH

Look out to the harmonies of the universe, and you will see beauty enfolding you. However, you will not find such beauty through mental gymnastics or analysis, but only if you listen to the sounds (not noises!)—the harmonies in the universal life. To get near to heaven, leave the lowlands and climb a hill or, better still, a mountain. Be alone, listening; observe the life of nature, and from outward recognition and realization of the universal life, look inwards. Try to realize the relationship between the outer mysteries and the life of the world within. When you stand alone in the silence of the open spaces, when you look into the heavens at the shining stars, you can feel an affinity, a brotherhood, a corresponding vibration of life.

All around you are the angels of light, the angels of nature. The great company of angels now encircles you, pouring upon you the radiance of their love, so that the light which is to be seen in the atoms of your physical, mental, astral and spiritual vehicles is quickened and illumined as you respond.

Leaving the city, we go into fields of wild flowers, see freshly shooting corn and trees laden with the early promise of fruit. We are conscious of the beauty of trees. Many people love to be alone and walk under the trees, or sit beneath them, and contemplate the sunlight ... and dream of life made radiant and beautiful.

The mystery schools of the past bring to us understanding of the wisdom of the sages of old, when they chose the trees as their cathedrals. In some quiet woodland, where a veritable natural cathedral has formed, have you not felt the sense of love and peace, and registered the blessing of these natural sanctuaries? There are many such cathedrals built by the tree spirits on the astral plane of life, where many weary souls coming from the earth can find refreshment and worship— not by word, but through the adoration and thankfulness of their hearts.

And so we come to the realization that the trees are symbolical to us of the Great Mother. In this realization we can walk in the groves, sit beneath the great oaks or an ancient banyan, or the majesty of the cedar, and become conscious of a mother-love enfolding us. And here you may draw very close to the earth angels; in the garden, where the flowers speak, the trees enfold you in friendliness and motherliness.

AFFIRMATIONS WITH THE EARTH ANGEL

I am as one with the Earth and
all her mysteries.

The angels of the Earth fill me with
their healing power.

All of nature surrounds and enfolds me.

*B*EYOND *the realms of the earth consciousness, we reach up to the spirits of the air, to
the sylphs and to the great air devas, who control the air currents, the storms and the winds.
When you hear the wind, just rejoice that you
are hearing the breath of God, experiencing the
power of the angels of the air.*

6

Angels of Air

CAN YOU recall the reaction upon your feelings or soul-body while listening to music that deeply moved you, or when you have listened to the wind in the trees? Do you then reach out and feel you touch something not purely physical, not only some vibration of the air?

How did music originate? We would suggest that it was by an effort to reproduce the sounds in the air created by the winds. And as you attune your hearing to these vibrations of sound, and reach behind the physical to the inner hearing, you will hear the mysterious word, the Creative Word pervading the air. The mysteries of this great Word of power shall be no longer mysteries.

The airy subjects are the true creators and inventors among people on the material plane. So also on the spiritual plane, the air beings are creators and receivers too—receivers of the messages from the higher angels. You can safely open your soul to their influences.

Can you feel the angelic presences? Can you feel their love and the purity of their souls? The air element is that of the true creative and receptive soul.

Yellow is the colour of the air element, the element which promotes communication of thought, of wisdom. Although one feels it to be a joyous, lively colour, as one discovers the essence of this yellow of wisdom, there is a stillness, a certainty. There is a faith in divine love. Yellow is the colour for those who need strengthening in faith and divine wisdom, and it is a good colour for those who are wrestling with mental problems. It can bring illumination. If you find yourself drawn to a clear yellow pool, your soul is reaching out towards divine wisdom.

The angels of wisdom are so still; the yellow is really the shining yellow-white of the sun's rays. It is the colour that we see so much in spring: the clear yellow of daffodils, forsythia, celandine and all the little golden flowers of spring. In the golden-yellow pool, see a silver-white fountain of light, like a flame, pure, cleansing, and yet so still! Rest in this flame and the answer to your problem will be made manifest. Because—make no mistake!—if you are true and fulfil your tasks, the angels will lead you on a golden path to a new way of life. We are only concerned with the spiritual evolution, the goodness, the happiness, the peace of all God's children on earth and in the spheres surrounding the earth. You are all one—and you are one with the angels.

As you unfold spiritually, you will be able to see, even as the ancients did, the spirits of the air, the sylphs and tiny fairies. You may go to some hilltop or mountain in a remote district and breathe in the sweetness of the air. If you are sensitive, you will feel something very beautiful. You will see in the skies countless millions of nature spirits, all working together for the good of life, and bringing gifts of food and sustenance to humanity.

We stand under the canopy of heaven, breathing in the air ... the life ... the peace of God. Let us raise our hearts to the love of the Infinite. We stand on the hilltop, amid trees and air, with the stars above ... and we are conscious of peace of soul.... We are inhaling the freshness and fragrance of the air of heaven. In these conditions we commune with the angels. The winds of heaven catch you and raise you up so that you may breathe in the breath of God, the inspiration of God. Behold now, a cloud of unseen witnesses is with you! See the radiant forms around you. See the forms of the angels draw close and become at one with you.

May your eyes be opened, may your senses realize the beauty of the unseen world about you....

THE PROCESS

This is a simple exercise. On rising, face the rising sun, if possible, before an open window (ideally, it would have been open all night). Stand erect so that you are correctly polarized, with the spine straight, the solar plexus controlled, heels together, toes slightly apart. Breathe naturally. But before you take your breath, centre your concentration—it will come in a flash—upon the central Light, the golden Light if you like.

You can realize this Light in your head centre. Now take your breath: on the first day, three; then six; then nine, and so on. And as you breathe, breathe into your solar plexus not only air, but life-atoms. Breathe them into your being. Raise your arms as you breathe in, if you find it helpful, and then, as you breathe out, let your arms fall slowly. You breathe in and absorb this stream of life and light from the angels of the air, and you let it fall from you in blessing upon others. So you absorb God's life, and you bless all life. You receive and you give; and so you come into harmony with the rhythmic lifestream. It will feed your nerves, and give you a sense of peace, and control.

AFFIRMATIONS WITH THE AIR ANGEL

I breathe in the divine breath of God.

*The angels of the air fill me with
their healing love.*

*The gentle breeze of heaven cools
and calms my spirit.*

*T*HE *angels of the fire element bring the divine
fire, the fire of love, of vision; it is through
their power that you develop that state of glorious
fire called love. Because of the angels of fire, love
illumines your heart and your life so that light goes
forth through the hands, through the mind, through
the emotions, through the speech: through every
action of life love flows out into the world. This
power is the same power that can create universes.
It can transform your life from darkness to light.*

7

Angels of Fire

THE WORLD of Fire is directly connected with the spiritual Sun power, and also with the heart and with the spirit. You know it by the solar force, the Sun light, the love within the human soul. Fire brings warmth and light and beauty into the life; light reveals the physical world to us. Fire gives us light; therefore we relate the element fire to the sense of sight.

In sight, you receive illumination of spirit. The light penetrates your inner being; and so, through the light of the Sun or the life spirit of the earth, your inner eyes may be opened so as to reveal the Light in all people.

Therefore you must have illumination in your own sight.... Your eyes being illumined—touched by the Divine Fire and Light—you see the beauty of all things.

We mean that when you sit devotedly in meditation and contemplation, and open your heart to the inflow of divine Love, you will be so raised in consciousness that you will behold the angels of the fire. You will reach a state of ecstasy and glory in which you will be in company with angels.

Let us consider the symbol of a lighted candle; the wick burns brightly, and little by little the wax around that flame dissolves and burns away. In a similar manner the flame of divine love by degrees consumes the lower self; it is transmuted and transformed. Love transforms life, removing all that is ugly and unwanted. What love does in life is to transform it.*

*This passage also appears in White Eagle's book INITIATIONS ON THE PATH OF THE SOUL.

Love is the fire, a great life force. If you feel this divine fire in your heart, it will come as strength. It will be to you like a rod of light. The soul who attains union with the Source of all being attains mastery over themselves, over life and over age. When a person understands how to keep attuned with the Source of all life, the physical body is renewed. This outpouring of golden light comes down and reaches you, if in simplicity you can open your heart to this blessing. It is like a spark which bursts into fire.

Remember that you hold within yourself that solar force. It is within you, buried deeply, and lies there sleeping. You can depend upon the angels to bring you divine fire, the healing power. When you realize that within you is the sun and centre of that force, you will then become not only healers of sick bodies but healers of nations, healers of life—animal life, vegetable life, physical life—and then healers of the soul and the mind, because this solar force works through all the planes surrounding the earth and all the bodies surrounding the physical body.

What do these words mean to you? Do they convey to you a fire of inspiration to go forth and seek and find, and to knock upon the door of the temple of initiation that you may be initiated into the greater mysteries and glories of the angelic kingdom?

May you and we be caught up in the fire of divine love, the Christ spirit, and be held forever in its heart!

CONTACTING THE ANGELS OF FIRE

We are not speaking of some nebulous force that you do not understand and you feel is very distant. This divine fire is within your very being and, as you raise your face to the sun, the rays of the sun stimulate this individual spark.

Keep your feet on the earth but lift your face towards the heavens, for the light which floods into you from on high will steady your feet and guide them in the right path. Have confidence in this divine light. Surrender with a tranquil mind and a heart full of love to this infinite wisdom.

We ask for the blessing of the glorious divine fire of the angels. As it flows into our hearts, we bow in humility and thankfulness for the gift of love. May we cause it to grow into a blazing fire within and without us, and may it leap from heart to heart in the world until at last humankind is united in one vast brother–sisterhood of the spirit.

THE PROCESS

Feel yourself bathing in a pool of sun-colour, rose red like the rising or setting sun, and feel the cleansing, healing power of the pool permeating your soul. It fills you with the divine energy—the aspiration, the strength, the joy, the courage, the creative warmth of the flame and the rose and orange rays.

These are the colours associated with the fire element, and with the angels of power and energy, and with that love which is a living creative power in the life, an inner flame of warmth and devotion. This type of love always shines in the aura as a warm rose pink and brings to the soul a fragrance, as of one of the old-fashioned roses warmed by the sun. It is a colour which brings healing balm. The warmth of the rose colour brings happiness, hope and creativity.

AFFIRMATIONS WITH THE FIRE ANGEL

*I open my heart to the divine fire of
love and the angels of fire.*

*I am surrounded by light. The light flows
through me, bringing healing to the world.*

*The angels of fire fill me with
warmth and happiness.*

*W*ATER, *being the first element, has a wonderful power and possesses wonderful properties on the spiritual and on the etheric plane. The water angels of the universe are connected with the water element in your own nature and also with your emotional reactions. They bring harmony and create peace and order.*

8

Angels of Water

THE WATER element is most important in the soul's spiritual development. The element of water is the basis of life, and every person must learn how to use this element, how to absorb it into their etheric body. Water possesses a special spiritual vibration. The psyche, or the psychic body, is very closely linked with the water element. Water is a purifier of the soul, the soul being the bridge between the physical body and the divine spirit. Once you have made this bridge, spirit messengers or angels are sent to you by the will of God. You are henceforth a channel, for you have opened the way for the creative power and light of the water angels to flow into you.

Water is the great lifegiver; had you no water, you would die. Try to understand it in this way: water is liquefied spirit. Then drink the water from a running brook, drink the sparkle and the sunlight which gives it life. Do you taste water only? No, more than water, we think: there is another indefinable, indestructible element to it. You drink the very life of the earth, take in a real part of the cosmic body, the life force. Through the water element you can create—or bring about in your physical body—both the turbulence of a storm and surpassing harmony and peace. Think well on this. Through the mouth, harmony and peace can enter—or instead, a tempest creating havoc in the physical body, just like a storm that whips up the ocean.

The Water initiation is meant to bring control of the emotions to the soul. The angels are unable to work with you if your emotions are like a turbulent sea. Do not shut them out. Stand by the side of a very still lake and look at the water, and see the reflection of the trees and the sky. How beautiful it is! But should that lake become ruffled, your reflection will be shattered. Take your eyes off the reflection in the water, however, and direct your vision to the true landscape—the trees and the skies as they are, and you will see something that is steady, clear, and to your sense, real.

You will know that there is water that is still and calm and which will reflect truth, and there is water which is so rough and turbulent that it cannot reflect the true image. Be calm. Be still. Do one thing at a time quietly, tranquilly, and you will make way in your soul for a great inflowing of spiritual power.

Now this is like a little spring of clear, life-giving water. We would liken all spiritual development to the beginning of the flowing river, the little spring which bubbles up from the earth and trickles down the hillside, growing broader and stronger and flowing faster sometimes as it travels, until it becomes a great river flowing onward to meet the ocean. The ocean may lie still and quiet; while standing alone in some quiet place, the soul can reach out and become conscious of the vastness, the depth and the profundity of life, the magnificence of the stillness and power of the sea. May the ocean speak to you of the eternal powers that lie within the creation of the universe. The waters enfold both man and woman in an enveloping yet impersonal peace ... in the grasp of an immense power.

CONTACTING THE ANGELS OF WATER

In your meditation, you may possibly see a pool or lake with lotus flowers upon its surface. Since water symbolizes the emotions, you learn by this scene that the emotions have to be stilled and controlled. If you look into still water, you will see a clear reflection of yourself and of anything else in your field of vision. If you look into water that is stirred up and troubled, you will see a distorted reflection. By this simple illustration, you learn the necessity of control and calmness of mind if you are going to see truth. Truth will only be revealed when there is stillness and peace.

Be still. Be at peace. With your imagination, project an image of the Star over the water. You are a focal point through which tremendous power and light works on earth. The angels of the water element, and those lesser spirits who work at their command, the water sprites, the undines: they work through you. When you offer healing, shoals of angelic beings come to you and carry from you the human love and the light which your love creates in the ether. These angelic beings come in vast numbers to carry the light

which you project and pour it over the place
or the condition that you name. This is how
the power works on the unseen planes.

THE PROCESS

We ask you to see with your inner vision what
we can see so clearly at the moment: a beautiful fountain here in the centre of our physical or spiritual Temple. It is rising from the
earth, shining in the light of the Star above;
and the rays of the Star and these streams of
water from the fountain are pouring down,
cleansing us, enfolding us. The light is danc-
ing on the falling water drops; they are almost
like gems of water. You are able to go to the
very heart of the fountain. Feel that you are
part of this fountain of light, cool, cleansing,
and powerful—but powerful in a very peaceful, beautiful way. Let us, for a few moments,
become part of this fountain of light, of pure

water, of spiritual power....

We are in the garden in the world of light. You can drink the water.... Do you see how the angels and indeed the spirits of the water element are all part of this great fountain, as we are?

And now there is a very beautiful feeling, an understanding that we are able to take a chalice of water and carry it to those who are thirsting, thirsting for the living waters....

AFFIRMATIONS WITH THE WATER ANGEL

I am divine calm. The turbulent seas within me lie still and peaceful.

The angels of water cleanse me with their healing power.

I flow with the conditions of my life.

*A*NGELIC *influences play upon us all, and it is well to understand that angels have important work for humanity. This present age of Aquarius will bring the angelic kingdom closer. Magic can be worked in our world by the cooperation and help of the angelic beings.*

9

Angels of the Planet

HUMANITY is guided and inspired by spirit beings. There are angel messengers who are drawn to the earth plane for different reasons, but mainly to assist the building up of the earth's evolution and to help to save humanity. Realize if you can the wonderful work that is going on, on the unseen planes. Great changes have come to humanity in the new age. The vibrational system of the earth is changing; the very substance of the earth is changing. Humanity's consciousness is gradually being raised to a plane of universal brotherhood. Though we live each in a certain country and of a certain nationality, yet as we evolve and raise our consciousness to the plane of pure spirit, or the divine life plane, there ceases to be separation. Instead, there is only the one vast universal brotherhood, such as will come eventually to all the earth.

You may think the world now is chaotic—but remember, a process of growth, the breaking, ploughing and cultivating of the seedbed, is taking place. The grand plan now goes forward, forward; and we would emphasize the wisdom of the angels who have the care of the earth life. You look out upon your world, you see its chaotic conditions and note that human life appears to be storm-tossed, and you wonder what will be the end. Behind every department of human life, behind politicians, statesmen and all the governments, there are greater minds working for the evolution of the race. And when you see what appears to you to be catastrophe, bear in mind that the Master mind is at work; and remember that the Masters and the angelic ones have a far deeper sympathy and love than you for all who suffer.

All creation is one vast brother–sisterhood of spirit, one atom inseparable from another. In this great family, all are held in the love and the power of the divine spirit. If only people on earth could raise their thoughts to the higher aspects, and realize the great beauty and the love which plans the progress and growth of the spirit of man and woman, then indeed the work of the Angel Ones would be greatly helped, as would the work of the older brethren who strive to bring light and love and joy into the hearts of their younger brethren.

The individual can do so much to help the angelic ones in their work of raising the vibrations of earth. The angels of light draw close to those who humbly and truly seek to serve the Great White Spirit. Service, when given freely and lovingly, when it transcends self, is inspired by the angels of light working through the soul. Once you have reached a certain stage of development, the curtain of the mists will be swept aside. Then will you see the glory of that rising sun and the company of the great beings, the angels—ageless beings waiting to welcome you into this new-born spiritual day.

You will walk and talk with angels—but remember that it takes an angel to recognize an angel, a god to recognize a god, so until you have developed the necessary qualities, you remain unconscious of the presence of angels or of gods. Do not think that you are far removed from such a grand spiritual experience, such ecstasy of being. You are not. Day by day you are approaching this illumination for which you must prepare in mind and in heart.

We visualize the grand brotherhood of humankind and angels in the spheres of light, and count no thing, no experience, useless; for we know that we journey on the path leading to the life of the spirit, the life eternal.

THE GREAT ANGELS

Open your consciousness to the ministering angels. We are taught by them not merely through words, but through the language of the spirit. A bridge between the higher worlds and the earth is built and angels cross this bridge to you. They can only cross it when you also ascend to the mountaintop—or, in other words, when you raise your consciousness so that the higher mind becomes receptive and absorbs spiritual truth and wisdom. You may carry with you an optimism—more than this, a positive knowledge, positive thought and positive action—as you journey through life, and thus train your spiritual hearing to catch the words of power and truth broadcast from the heights.

We want you to understand how closely you are all bound up with the betterment of the earth planet and the unfoldment of humanity. You must believe and know that none can live to himself or herself alone, and that your thoughts, your way of life, your service, are all contributing to the angels a quality which they use to help urge the whole of humankind forward. If you doubt whether your efforts have any effect upon your fellow beings in the present day, we assure you that it is only through such efforts throughout the ages that the world is still progressing and humanity is still living and enjoying life. In spite of all the warlike destruction, behind the veil are the angelic beings labouring ceaselessly to influence and help your world to better things.

You are likely to come within the influence of these beings in your daily life; at the moment you do not know it, but if you cultivate your soul qualities, if your life contributes helpfulness and kindliness to all, you are developing a light within which will shine forth from your head and your heart, drawing the angels to you. Cultivate a sense of peace, recognizing at all times the angelic organization behind the scenes, working always to bring the world to perfection.

AFFIRMATIONS WITH THE ANGEL OF THE WORLD

I work with the angels to bring healing to all countries of the world.

I serve humanity, hand in hand with angels.

I open my heart and my mind to the angelic influences that are working for peace.

*H*UMANITY *is one vast brotherhood of life, and you are part of the whole of creation. All nature is part of you; you are part of nature.*

May your eyes be open so that you see the host of heavenly ones, angels who are real beings, who love and serve God in the heavens and every living creature on this earth.

10

Angels of the Nature Kingdoms

THE BROTHERHOOD of all life consists of human beings, the animal kingdom, the nature world, the spirit world, the angelic kingdoms and all the natural elements. The normal man or woman sees only the physical manifestation of life and ignores the intelligence behind the form, the beauty of which brings to him or her so much joy. Behind every manifestation in physical matter, there exist both on the etheric and on the higher planes (astral, mental and spiritual) further forms of life.

The angelic line of service is concerned with life in form throughout every stream of life in the nature kingdom. You are part of the animal kingdom; you are part of the air and the birds in the air and the fish in the sea. Each one has, attached to it, an angelic being, or beings. The lower angels watch over the lower life forms on earth, and the tiny spirits, ever at work, are animated by the thought power of the lower angels, and so are more or less thought forms. Some people call them elementals. When their work is finished, they quietly fade away. Not all 'fairies' are like this; some are lasting creations on their own line of evolution, and work upwards and merge eventually into the angelic kingdom.

A process of spiritual growth and harmony is working throughout the universe. All we can do is to appreciate that behind all physical form is this wonderful and beautiful, invisible etheric life. When we thus open our vision to see the angels at work and view the glorious panorama of God's love, God's beauty manifest everywhere, we shall help the whole. You, as a brother or a sister of the universal life, have your work to do to swell the great orchestra of nature. You must love nature and strive to become aware of the life behind the form, to be more kind in your treatment of all growing things, to love all living manifestations of the God-life.

When humankind learn the secrets of nature's mysteries they will no longer proceed on the path of domination, but will work on cooperating with these angelic beings and the hosts of nature spirits who work under the angels' direction. To contact that inner world of angelic beings you must learn self-mastery and harmony.

CONTACTING THE ANGELS
OF THE NATURE KINGDOMS

Some will take a country walk and see very little. They stay unaware of the beauties of nature. They have not reflected their surroundings. Others will take that same walk and become aware of maybe a thousand little details apparent to them in the hedgerow and fields, in the bird life, in the sunlight, in the shadow, and in the atmosphere—many details they will note. They are not merely observant with the physical eye, but with the spiritual eye also. Conceive yet others taking that same walk. They have become more sensitive still to the spiritual life behind the physical form, and their sight again has greatly increased. They will not only see all the details of a physical nature, but also become aware of the pulsation or vibration of life and great beauty which permeates the physical manifestation. Their souls will reflect the spirit world.

Recreation should be purposeful. You must use the time at your disposal to the best possible advantage. If you have a period of relaxation, completely relax your body and your mind and give yourself up to the revivifying spiritual forces. Enjoy your rest, be filled with sunlight, enjoy nature, lie upon mother earth and absorb the magnetism of the earth. Breathe in the air and glorify it: glory in it.

THE PROCESS

In the midst of nature, if you can shut out all earthly sounds and enter into the innermost part of yourself, you will hear sounds—or music, harmonics—and you will get beneath physical sounds, and hear the deep musical harmony of nature—but nature within nature. In that music, nature spirits have being; these sounds quicken their life force, and enable them to receive instruction from their god. That is not the great Father-Mother, but the one at the head of the ray upon which they live, who is part of the Whole. The song of birds consists of the vibrations which assist them to bring forth the fruits of the earth. We also become aware of this same principle in nature.

In simplicity we pray that nature in all its beauty shall convey to our waiting hearts some of the inner mystery of life. We lift our hearts to the hills, to the mountains, to the windswept skies; we touch the rain-drenched earth, we see the beauty and power of nature. We worship the grandeur and glory of our Creator's handiwork and, becoming in tune with the infinite Spirit, we awaken to the beauty within ourselves. We yearn to become united in fuller consciousness with the glory of God our Father–Mother. In this grand Brotherhood, may we learn to fold to our breasts our brethren of the human and animal kingdoms.

May all fear leave us, and may we know love and beauty and peace....

AFFIRMATIONS WITH THE ANGELS OF NATURE

*I open my senses to the
glorious beauty of nature.*

*I work with the angels of nature
to bring healing to the earth.*

*The harmonious power of the
universe shines through me.*

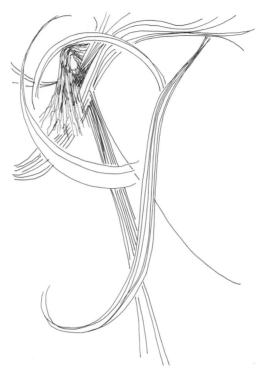

*T*HE *angelic kingdom helps to create form, to bring inspiration in music and art to human life. Form ... colour ... sound ... vibration: all these contain the white magic of the creative force.*

11

Angels of Music

WHEN YOU listen to beautiful music, you are perhaps unaware of what is being created. You love harmony; you enjoy music and rhythm with your mind—it does something to your being. But few people understand the real influence of music. When you listen to music that you enjoy, remember that the music is drawing angels of music who have work to do with the evolution of humanity. In religion, we find angels working through ceremony and form to distribute the force, the power, the God life among us, thus helping us to expand and grow.

Beautiful music, built on a harmony

which raises the soul, draws to the musician and those participating certain angelic beings whose glory it is impossible to describe. The angels of music are concerned with the creation of the form and sound of music and so help to bring music forth from silence into sound, so that the body and spirit may hear the divine harmonies. The listener may be caught up, be bathed in the aura of these glorious ones. Oh, how difficult is it to come down to earth again! To mix again with the harsh vibrations of ordinary life is painful after the soul has been raised to heights through the ritual of the musician.

Conceive passing through that babble—inharmonious, crude and harsh, through that plane close to the physical—and reaching upwards through the planes of spiritual life! Each plane is more harmonious and gentle until we reach the spheres of absolute harmony. On these planes there is music in the atmosphere. The very clothing of the inhabitants vibrates harmony and music. And you may acquire the power to tune into that divine orchestra. But this is not merely a physical gift, it is a soul gift, and it lies within you. You may acquire the power to hear more clearly and correctly than you can hear the music on the physical plane. But first there must be harmony. There must be purity and there must be love within.

Do not live entirely shut up in your closed physical brain, because there are other cells in it which are as yet unused. They will develop as humanity searches for harmony, for love, for God in life. Then the brain cells will be stimulated and become receptive to spiritual waves; they will be able to hear heavenly music. More than this, they will hear the heavenly message.

There is nothing like harmonious music for creating harmony in a soul. In the new age, sound and music play a very big part. Sound and music provoke feeling; through feeling and imagination you develop gifts of the spirit, yet feeling and imagination are the very qualities which so many human people need help to develop. This is why beautiful music is a necessity in our work. It can contribute to the awakening and development of the man or woman's feeling for God, and to feelings of Christ's presence. The Christ qualities in the human soul are awakened when the soul hears beautiful sound. The music of the heavens can be heard and the angelic choir is singing praises and thanksgiving to God.

OPENING YOUR EARS TO THE ANGELIC MUSIC

When you learn to withdraw from the noise and bustle of the world, so that you may enter into your own inner sanctuary, you will develop that sensitive hearing which will enable you to hear the music of nature, the music of the tiniest bird, the music which is in the air. Just think of it: to be able to hear the music which is in the rippling water, in the gentle breeze, the shaking of the leaves of the trees!

In the silence, you listen ... and begin to hear the music of heavenly spheres, the music of nature, of the wind in the trees, the song of the birds, the gentle murmur of the voices of the ferns and flowers, and even the murmur of the blades of grass. You must learn to be still and listen to God's voice, which is showing that all are one in the spirit—*one*. You are surrounded by the angels. You may not be able to see them, but you may be able to feel them. They are with you, in the quiet of your own innermost being.

THE PROCESS

When sound is sent forth from a physical instrument, you may be able to see very beautiful colours emerging. Practise seeing how the colours are created from the sound of beautiful and harmonious music—strong and powerful when the music is strong and powerful, soft and gentle when the music is quiet.

Then, listen quietly and intensely to catch the music of life, the music which is so healing, so harmonious. We see that through the music you have heard, the angels of music are drawn close to serve you, touching your souls as hands play upon a harp, so that you also may absorb the harmony of the spheres of music.

Imagine yourself in the spheres of perfect harmony; and listen to the divine music of the great orchestra of the angels—and see intermingling with the angelic forms, the most beautiful colours, vibrant and creating life.... It is impossible to give you more!

AFFIRMATIONS WITH THE ANGELS OF MUSIC

I open my hearing to the music of the angels.

*My life is harmonious. I am in
harmony with God.*

I listen to the music of life.

12

Epilogue:
An Attunement
in the Angelic Temple

LET US raise our consciousness, away from the confused turmoil and clamour of the physical life and up into the heavenly consciousness of God and God's angels. We will open our hearts to the inflow of the love and peace and power of all the angels of the celestial spheres, the angels of the elements. Let us raise our thoughts again to the Great White Light, and may the angels of love, the angels of wisdom and the angels of power guide us onward and upward in the glories of the Light!

Imagine that blazing golden Sun. Even doing this immediately raises you up from the greyness of earth to the glory of the heavens. Imagine that you are looking into heaven through a golden gate. This opens, and you see beyond a company of shining forms. We see the great canopy of white wings, living wings, pulsating wings, pulsating with light all over this shrine, this temple in the spirit world. We are right up in the mountaintop, and the air we breathe is pure and fresh. As we enter the portals of the temple, on either side like two pillars stand two angels ... and as we pass them we are offered the cup of pure water, the grail cup.

Sip, sip the water of life, the healing water, and enter this holy place, where we are in a golden world, and we see all round in a circle these angel forms with wings of light, beautiful faces, all so perfectly peaceful and joyous. You can feel the joy, you can feel the peace, you feel your troubles and your heaviness all falling away. We look about us, and that dome of wings is supported by tall pillars of light, and each pillar is a great healing angel.

You will see the most delicate colours of the rainbow, moving, vibrating, in beautifully soft, billow-like clouds. The angelic beings are still; and are directing rays of light which go forth from their heads, from their aura. They are not disturbed by any world problem. They know one truth: that all is working together for good. They come to help humanity realize this grand truth.... All is working together for good. Get above fear thought; get beyond and above, and live in the positive thought of good becoming manifest on all planes of being.

This should be the prayer of every aspirant on the path of light, because only when the soul becomes truly humble can it be receptive to the guidance, help and love of the invisible brethren and the angelic messengers who wait under God's command to come to you and to all human beings. Remember that the key which unlocks the door to these heavenly mysteries lies not in the human mind but in the heart. Truth is simple, and because it is so simple it is hidden from those who have great knowledge and powerful intellects, or those who play with words. They wait, but it is revealed to the loving heart.